P!nk

KIRKLEES Culture and Leisure Services

I'm Not Dead

Piano • Vocal • Guitar

...es   Culture & Leisure Services
Red Do' Lane
..ld, West Yo...

ISBN 13: 978-1-4234-1506-0
ISBN 10: 1-4234-1506-X

HAL•LEONARD®
CORPORATION

7777 W. BLUEMOUND RD. P.O. BOX 13819 MILWAUKEE, WI 53213

In Australia Contact:
Hal Leonard Australia Pty. Ltd.
4 Lentara Court
Cheltenham, Victoria, 3192 Australia
Email: ausadmin@halleonard.com

Visit Hal Leonard Online at
www.halleonard.com

800138552

Songs

STUPID GIRLS

Words and Music by ALECIA MOORE,
BILLY MANN, NIKLAS OLOVSON
and ROBIN LYNCH

Moderately, with a beat

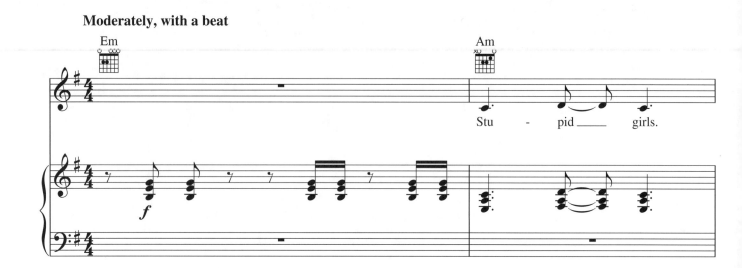

Stu - pid ___ girls.

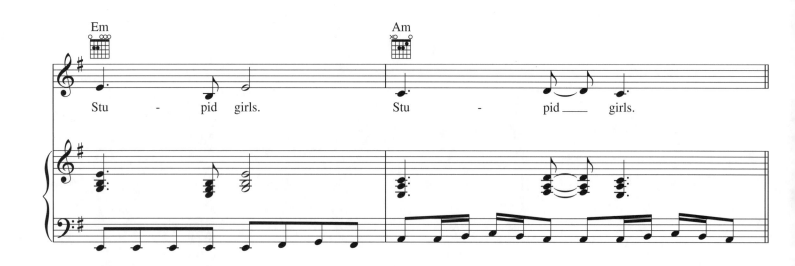

Stu - pid girls. Stu - pid ___ girls.

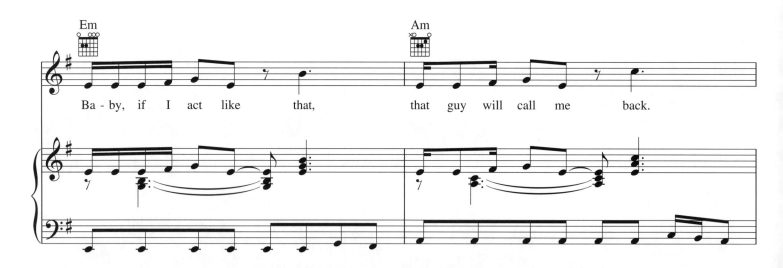

Ba - by, if I act like that, that guy will call me back.

What a pa-pa-raz-zi girl. I don't wan-na be a stu-pid girl.

Go to Fred Se-gal, you'll find 'em there. Laugh-in' loud so all the lit-tle peo-ple stare.

Look-in' for a dad-dy to pay for the cham-pagne. Drop a name. What

like this, like this. Pret-ty will you fuck me girl. Sil-ly as a luck-y girl.

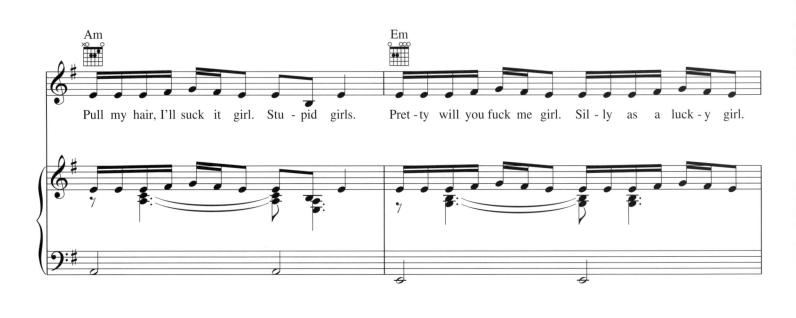

Pull my hair, I'll suck it girl. Stu-pid girls. Pret-ty will you fuck me girl. Sil-ly as a luck-y girl.

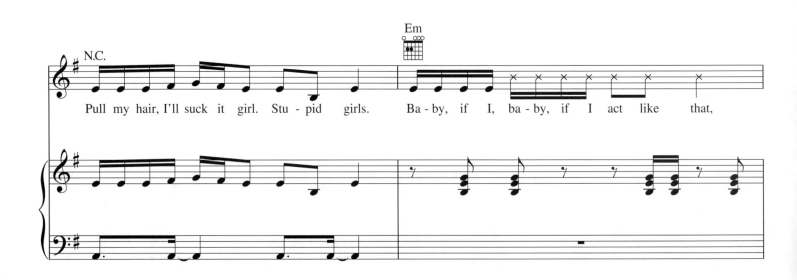

Pull my hair, I'll suck it girl. Stu-pid girls. Ba-by, if I, ba-by, if I act like that,

WHO KNEW

Words and Music by ALECIA MOORE,
MAX MARTIN and LUKASZ GOTTWALD

Vocal is written one octave higher than sung.

20

My dar - ling, my dar - ling, who _ knew?

My dar - ling, I miss _ you, my dar - ling.

Who _ knew?

Who ___ knew?

LONG WAY TO HAPPY

Words and Music by ALECIA MOORE
and BUTCH WALKER

Lead vocal is written one octave higher than sung.

NOBODY KNOWS

Words and Music by ALECIA MOORE
and BILLY MANN

DEAR MR. PRESIDENT

Words and Music by ALECIA MOORE
and BILLY MANN

I'M NOT DEAD

Words and Music by ALECIA MOORE
and BILLY MANN

Lead vocal is written one octave higher than sung.

CUZ I CAN

Words and Music by ALECIA MOORE,
MAX MARTIN and LUKASZ GOTTWALD

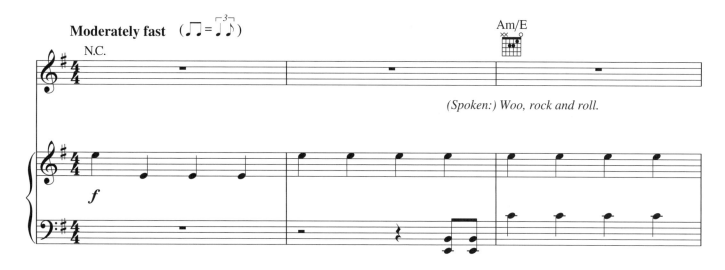

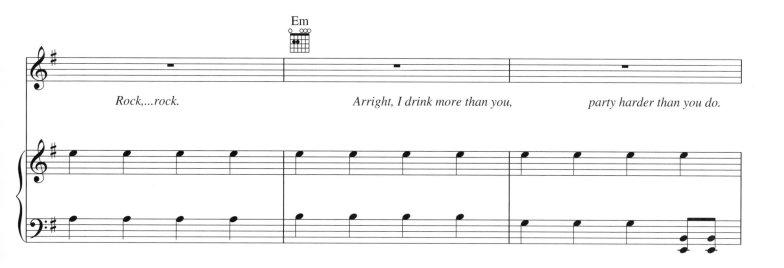

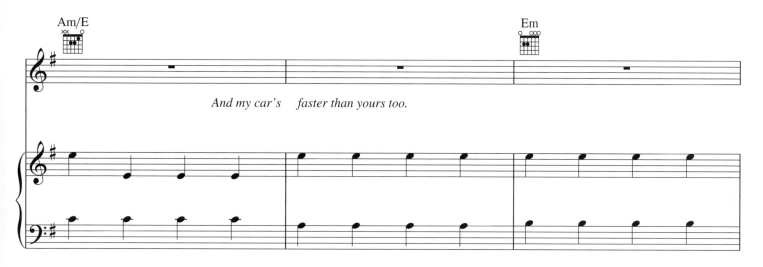

Lead vocal is written one octave higher than sung.

LEAVE ME ALONE
(I'm Lonely)

Words and Music by ALECIA MOORE
and BUTCH WALKER

U & UR HAND

Words and Music by ALECIA MOORE,
MAX MARTIN, LUKASZ GOTTWALD and RAMI

Vocal line is written one octave higher than sung.

RUNAWAY

Words and Music by ALECIA MOORE
and BILLY MANN

*Vocal line written one octave higher than sung.

84

THE ONE THAT GOT AWAY

Words and Music by ALECIA MOORE
and BILLY MANN

I stood by the ex-it door in the ho-tel ca-fé. He was

play-ing with his band. I've al-ways been a suck-er, had a weak-

ness for a boy with a gui-tar and a drink in his hand. His

I GOT MONEY NOW

Words and Music by ALECIA MOORE
and MICHAEL ELIZONDO

CONVERSATIONS WITH MY 13 YEAR OLD SELF

Words and Music by ALECIA MOORE
and BILLY MANN